# The Godly Man Curriculum
## Course Workbook

The Godly Man Curriculum Course Workbook
Published by Guy Thing Press
P.O. Box 827
Roanoke, TX 76262

This book or parts thereof may not be reproduced in any form, stored in a retrieval system, or transmitted in any form by any means—electronic, mechanical, photocopy, recording, or otherwise—without prior written permission of the publisher, except as provided by United States of America copyright law.

Guy Thing Press books may be purchased in bulk for educational, business, fund-raising, or sales promotional use. For more information, please contact Guy Thing Press.

Please visit us at www.guythingpress.com

Unless otherwise noted, scripture taken from the HOLY BIBLE, NEW INTERNATIONAL VERSION®. Copyright © 1973, 1978, 1984 International Bible Society. Used by permission of Zondervan. All rights reserved.

Copyright © 2007 by Dr. John A. King
All rights reserved

*Printed in the United States of America*

ISBN-13: 978-0-9818337-0-5
ISBN-10: 0-9818337-0-5

# Table of Contents

### Unit 1 - What We Believe

| | | |
|---|---|---|
| 1.1 | Faith Toward God | 5 |
| 1.2 | What We Believe Part 1 | 17 |
| 1.3 | What We Believe Part 2 | 25 |

### Unit 2 - The Heart of a Man

| | | |
|---|---|---|
| 2.1 | God and Man | 31 |
| 2.2 | Heroes | 37 |

### Unit 3 - Your Word is Your Bond

| | | |
|---|---|---|
| 3.1 | Your Word | 41 |
| 3.2 | Your Word and Your Family | 45 |

### Unit 4 - A Place to Belong

| | | |
|---|---|---|
| 4.1 | A Fresh Definition of Church Part 1 | 49 |
| 4.2 | A Fresh Definition of Church Part 2 | 53 |
| 4.3 | Why Should We Fellowship? | 57 |

### Unit 5 - The Imitation of Christ

| | | |
|---|---|---|
| 5.1 | The Imitation of Christ's Humility Part 1 | 61 |
| 5.2 | The Imitation of Christ's Humility Part 2 | 65 |
| 5.3 | The Imitation of Christ's Generosity | 69 |

## Unit 6 - Creating a Better Life

| | | |
|---|---|---|
| 6.1 | Key #1 | 73 |
| 6.2 | Key #2 | 77 |
| 6.3 | Key #3 | 81 |

## Unit 7 - Character is King

| | | |
|---|---|---|
| 7.1 | Created for Excellence | 85 |
| 7.2 | Faithfulness - The Very Character of God | 89 |
| 7.3 | God Has Anointed You For Business | 93 |

## Unit 8 - Marriage and Family

| | | |
|---|---|---|
| 8.1 | Different From the Start | 97 |
| 8.2 | The Sacredness of Sex | 101 |
| 8.3 | What's the Big Deal With Pornography? | 107 |
| 8.4 | The Process of Pornography | 111 |
| 8.5 | Freedom From the Effects of Pornography | 115 |
| 8.6 | Fatherhood | 119 |
| 8.7 | Six Keys to Raising Children | 127 |
| 8.8 | Seven Keys to Family Discipline | 131 |
| 8.9 | Creating Your Child's Character | 135 |

## Unit 9 - Achieving Authentic Wealth

| | | |
|---|---|---|
| 9.1 | Preparing For Wealth | 139 |
| 9.2 | Multiplying Money Into Wealth | 143 |
| 9.3 | How To Lose Your Wealth | 147 |
| 9.4 | The Real Purpose of Wealth | 151 |
| 9.5 | Consider Abraham Part 1 | 155 |
| 9.6 | Consider Abraham Part 2 | 159 |
| 9.7 | Consider Abraham Part 3 | 163 |

# Session 1-1
# WHAT WE BELIEVE
## Faith Toward God

# What We Believe
## Session 1: Faith Toward God

Faith toward God is the second of the six foundation stones listed in Hebrews 6:1-2.

# I. Let's start with a: DEFINITION OF FAITH

**A. Faith is first a _____; it is more then just a mental _____.**

A person who has faith believes something _____. He has total confidence in God and trusts that His promises will come true.

> *Hebrews 11:1*
> *"Now faith is the substance of things hoped for, the evidence of things not seen"*

**B. Faith requires _____ in obedience to God's Word.**

When God commands a person to do something, he may not always understand why. In fact, it may not make any sense at all. But God wants you to step out by faith in obedience to Him, knowing that His way is perfect.

> *Acts 6:7*
> *"Then the word of God spread, and the number of the disciples multiplied greatly in Jerusalem, and a great many of the priests were _____"*

# II. THE IMPORTANCE OF FAITH

**A. Faith is important because it is the _____ of the entire Christian life.**

> *Hebrews 11:6*
> *"But without faith it is impossible to please Him, for he who comes to God must believe that He is, and that He is a rewarder of those who diligently seek Him."*

## B. You cannot know God without _____.

Nothing can be known or received of God unless man first _____ and also that God has revealed Himself in His Word, the Bible.

*Romans 1:16,17*
*"For I am not ashamed of the gospel of Christ, for it is the power of God to salvation for everyone who believes. For in it the righteousness of God is _____."*

# III. THE SOURCE OF FAITH

_____ is the source of our faith.

1. **Faith, like all other good gifts we receive, comes from above.**

   **Look up and write out the following scriptures:**

   *John 3:27*
   _____
   _____
   _____

   *James 1:17*
   _____
   _____
   _____

   *Eph. 2:8*
   _____
   _____
   _____

**2.** Faith is not the result of our own will or ability. God gives us the ability to exercise faith through the Holy Spirit.

*John 1:12,13*
*"But as many as received Him, to them He _____ to become children of God, to those who believe in His name: who were born, not of blood, nor of the will of the flesh, nor of the will of man, but of God."*

## B. The Word of God is the _____ of this faith, which is available to everyone.

*Romans 10:17*
*"So then faith comes by hearing, and hearing by the word of God."*

Faith is not based upon what you say or how you say it, but based upon what God has _____.

## C. Faith comes out of _____.

To have faith in God means to have trust in God. You can transpose the word faith for the word trust anywhere in the N.T. and not change the original meaning of the scripture.

The word faith in the Greek means:
_____

It stems from another Greek word which means:
_____

*Romans 1:17*
*"For in it the righteousness of God is revealed from faith to faith; as it is written, "The just shall live by faith."*

Confidence and trust in what?
That Jesus is who He says He is and can do what He said He can do. Trust and confidence come out of _____, and _____ is intimacy over time.

So relationship with God and knowledge of God are our greatest source of faith. In fact the only source of our trust is our faith. The whole basis of our developing faith is our developing relationship with God.

## D. Faith is a Fruit

**Write out** *Galatians 5:22:*

_____

_____

A fruit is something you can grow. Apples are the natural by-product of a healthy Apple tree. Faith is the natural by-product of healthy Christian walk. As you sink your roots deep into the soil of the Word, watering it with His spirit, you will bear the fruit of faith.

# IV. WHO HAS FAITH?

## A. All believers have been given _____ by God.

In Romans 12, Paul is clearly addressing Christians.

> *Romans 12:3*
> *"For I say, through the grace given to me, to everyone who is among you, not to think of himself more highly than he ought to think, but to think soberly, as God has dealt to each one a _____ _____."*

The "everyone" refers to every _____.

In line with this calling, with God's destiny there is a set portion of faith, the amount that fits us for the task ahead, given to us to do what needs to be done for the Glory of God and the expansion of His kingdom.

## B. _____ do not have faith.

It is true that all men have the capacity to give intellectual assent to Scripture, but this is not saving faith. Even demons are wise enough to intellectually acknowledge Jesus as Lord, but they are incapable of exercising saving faith in God.

Those that don't know Christ may take on a form of godliness, but by their _____ and _____ they deny the _____ of it's _____.

They may apply biblical principals and live according to biblical ethics, but that is not the same as acknowledging God for who He is.

# V. OBEDIENCE TO FAITH

Faith is an attitude of _____, _____ and _____ God.

The source of this faith and this trust is God Himself, and He has generously made faith available to all believers through His Word, the Bible.

According to His Word, faith is much more than a passive, inactive condition of the mind.

Faith requires acting upon one's _____. Faith requires obedience to our _____.

### A. The Word of God is usually communicated in terms of _____.

Commands are central to the preaching of Jesus and the apostles:

"Rise and walk",
"Receive your sight",
"Zaccheus... come down",
"Lazarus come forth"

Having faith involves believing God's Word and then stepping out and doing it. Taking action based upon confidence and trust.

### B. "Disbelieve" = _____

"Disbelieve" and "disobey" in the original Greek are used interchangeably, suggesting that if one really believes God's Word, then he will naturally and automatically obey it.

Not believing what God says is actually disobedience, and disobedience is sin.

**Write out** *Hebrews 3:18,19*

_____
_____
_____

## Lesson 1-1
## What We Believe 1 - Faith Toward God

Your lack of action is an indication of your lack of trust. To have faith in God is to have trust in God.

**C. "Obedience to faith" is the natural _____ of early believers in Christ.**

*Acts 6:7*
*"Then the word of God spread, and a great many of the priests were _____ to the faith."*

*Romans 1:5 and 16:26*
*"Through Him we have received grace and apostleship for _____ to the faith among all nations for His name," according to the commandment of the everlasting God, for obedience to the faith— "*

There is a living faith, but there is also a dead faith.
A Faith without _____,
A Faith without _____,
A Faith without _____,
Is a dead faith.

Praying for the sick by most people is dead faith. Why?
_____
_____
_____

Praying for someone's salvation is mostly dead faith. Why?
_____
_____
_____

Don't waste your time and air if you're not going to make the effort to put faith into action.

## Please stop here to complete questions 1-4

**1.** Explain how faith is more than just a mental attitude.

_____
_____
_____

**2.** Give two specific examples from Scripture where actions were necessary in obedience to faith.

_____
_____
_____

**3.** In your own words, explain the relationship between "belief" and "obedience".

_____
_____
_____

**4.** Read James 2:17, 18. According to James, what is the best way to show that you have faith?

_____
_____
_____

So now we understand that faith is from God; that we are each given a measure of faith to which we must be obedient, but what about the whole concept of growing in our faith.

# VI. FOUR HINDRANCES TO FAITH

**A. _____, in other words engaging in non-godly things, is the easiest way to hinder your faith.**

> *Galatians 5:17-21*
> *"For the flesh lusts against the Spirit, and the Spirit against the flesh; and these are contrary to one another, so that you do not do the things that you wish. But if you are led by the Spirit, you are not under the law. Now the works of the flesh are evident, which are: adultery, fornication, uncleanness,*

## Lesson 1-1
## What We Believe 1 - Faith Toward God

*lewdness, idolatry, sorcery, hatred, contentions, jealousies, outbursts of wrath, selfish ambitions, dissensions, heresies, envy, murders, drunkenness, revelries, and the like; of which I tell you beforehand, just as I also told **you** in time past, that those who practice such things will not inherit the kingdom of God. "*

### B. Neglect of the _____ will hinder your faith.

*Galatians 6:7,8*
*"Do not be deceived, God is not mocked; for whatever a man sows, that he will also reap. For he who sows to his flesh will of the flesh reap corruption, but he who sows to the Spirit will of the Spirit reap everlasting life."*

### C. Neglect of the promises of the _____ will hinder faith.

*Hebrews 2:1*
*"Therefore we must give the more earnest heed to the things we have heard, lest we drift away."*

### D. Disobedience to the _____ that God has revealed will hinder faith.

Remember that "obedience to faith" is what faith is all about; one must do what God shows him to do.

*James 2:17*
*"Thus also faith by itself, if it does not have works, is dead."*

You are accountable for the truth that has been revealed. If you cannot be faithful in the little things, don't waste your breath praying for great things. Be faithful to your current revelation – the thing God has called you to. This is the foundation upon which He is establishing your tomorrow.

## Stop here to do questions 5-7

**5.** List all of the fruits or evidence of the flesh found in Galatians 5:17-21

_____
_____
_____

**6.** Why is it important to walk in the Spirit?

_____
_____
_____

**7.** According to Jude 20, how can you build yourself on "the most holy faith"?

_____
_____
_____

## Lesson 1-1
### What We Believe 1 - Faith Toward God

# Written Essay.
## Please answer each question individually or as a complete essay

**1.** Using Scripture references, explain where faith originates and how you as a believer can obtain it.

**2.** What does it mean to be "obedient to the faith"? Are You?

**3.** In your own life, how can you tell when you are "walking in the Spirit" instead of "walking in the flesh"?

**4.** Do you ever neglect the Word? Why is it extremely important to stay in the Word?

# Session 1-2
# WHAT WE BELIEVE
## Hell Yeah

# What We Believe
## Session 2: Hell Yeah

*Luke 10:18 And He said to them, "I saw Satan fall like lightning from heaven."*

Our views and our understanding of both heaven and hell are based upon _____ and _____ as opposed to biblical fact and doctrine.

*A man can no more diminish God's glory by refusing to worship Him than a lunatic can put out the sun by scribbling the word 'darkness' on the walls of his cell.*

*God cannot give us a happiness and peace apart from Himself, because it is not there. There is no such thing.*

*C. S. Lewis*

The greatest trick the devil ever pulled was to convince the world that he does not exist or that he is just a benign object of our amusement.

In the USA _____% of people believe in heaven. _____% believe in hell

Yet _____% reject the existence of Satan and only _____% expects to go to hell.

We feel comfortable with the thoughts of the rewards, but not with the thoughts of the consequence of our actions.

We live in a society where comfort is our aim and we legislate against the consequence of our action. In fact, 75% of Americans believe in moral relativism, in other words _____.
Allow your _____ to guide your conduct as opposed to allow your _____ to form the construct for your behavior

You cannot come to an understanding of _____, without an understanding of _____.

## Summary:

The Scriptures teach the existence of Satan who is _____ of sin and the king over a host of fallen angels and spirits who carry out his work.

Christ conquered Satan and the kingdom of darkness at Calvary and commissioned the Church to deliver men from it and bring them into the _____.

# Lesson 1-2
## What We Believe 2 - Hell Yeah

The ultimate judgment of Satan and his forces will be when they are cast into the Lake of Fire for eternity. Jesus Himself, before the beginning of time, saw Satan fall. The character of any kingdom is reflected in the _____ of the king.

Satan's kingdom, the kingdom of darkness is diametrically _____ to the kingdom of God in _____, _____ and _____. Jesus said that Satan came to _____, _____ and _____. But that He came so that we could have abundant life.

**Fill in the aspects of each kingdom below:**

| Satan's Kingdom | God's Kingdom |
|---|---|
|  |  |
|  |  |
|  |  |
|  |  |
|  |  |

Believers today either _____ Satan's existence and power or _____ it. These extremes come from lack of knowledge. People don't understand what they don't know.

# Who is Satan?

In the spaces below, list the characteristics of Satan:

_____     _____
_____     _____
_____     _____
_____     _____
_____     _____
_____     _____
_____     _____

**His name reveals his nature and character:**

His many names denote his personality characteristics.

**Satan** means: _____

**Devil** means: _____

**Serpent/Dragon** means: _____
_____

**Antichrist** means: _____

**Fowler** means: _____

**His character dictates his activities.**

The majority of Satan's activities are centered on _____.

It should be understood that Satan's activities are limited. Although he is mighty, he is not All-mighty, Although he is powerful, he is not all-powerful, nor is he omnipresent – he can't be everywhere at once.

## Lesson 1-2
## What We Believe 2 - Hell Yeah

**The activities of Satan can be grouped into seven main areas:**

1. _____ .

2. _____ or rebellion against divine authority.

3. _____ This is his greatest power and the first weapon used in the garden and it is his last days weapons against the nations of the earth.

4. _____ These are against the saints, but as believers we can thank God that we have an advocate in Christ Jesus.

5. _____ He seeks to afflict physically and mentally.

6. _____ He and his army is in a war against God and His kingdom.

7. _____ This is the greatest power of Satan manifest, but Jesus conquered its power through His resurrection.

# Satan's fall

What caused Satan's fall?

_____
_____
_____
_____
_____

What will God hold man eternally accountable for?

_____
_____
_____
_____

# Lets talk about Hell

According to the lesson, what is the purpose of Hell?

_____

_____

Hell was not made for _____ and _____ was not made for hell.

Who was Hell created for?

_____

## Hell is described in the Bible as a place of:

- _____ *(Matt 7:3)*
- _____ *(Rom 2:6)*
- _____ *(Matt 25:46)*
- _____ *(Matt 8:12)*
- _____ *(Mark 9:43)*
- _____ *(Matt 13:42)*
- _____ *(2 Thess 1:9)*
- _____
  _____ *(Matt 5:29)*
- _____ *(Matt 13:42)*
- _____ *(Rev 14:9)*

  and _____ *(Mark 9:43)*
- _____
  _____ *(Is 66:22, Rev 14:9, Is 65:17)*

## Lesson 1-2
## What We Believe 2 - Hell Yeah

When humanity stopped believing in creation, they stopped believing that they were made in God's image, and, in turn, they attempted to recast God in their own image.

- A god of _____.

- A god that _____.

- A god that never _____ or _____.

- A god that accepts _____.

Why do some people not like the idea of God?

_____
_____

**How have we redefined God?**

_____
_____
_____
_____

What was the purpose of the 10 Commandments?

_____
_____

The consequence of not submitting to God is _____.

What is repentence?

_____

_____


An honest examination of scripture shows us that hell is a place of_____.

- He destroyed the power of _____, that is the devil *(Heb 2:14)*
- He was raised up having defeated _____ and _____ *(Acts 2:24)*
- But if the Spirit of Him who raised Jesus from the dead dwells in you, He who raised Christ from the dead will also _____ to your mortal bodies through His Spirit who dwells in you. *(Romans 8:11)*

# Session 1-3
# WHAT WE BELIEVE
## Resurrection of the Dead

# What We Believe
## Session 3: Resurrection of the Dead

## I. The Central Theme

_____ is the central theme of the Gospel of Jesus Christ. It is important to realize that the resurrection of Christ provided more than a _____ and _____ basis for the Christian faith.

Write out the following scriptures:

Colossians 2:13

_____
_____
_____
_____

Hebrews 6:1, 2

_____
_____
_____
_____

### A. A New Concept

Although the Jews believed in the resurrection, what did they not relate to it?

_____
_____

# Lesson 1-3
## What We Believe 3 - Resurrection of the Dead

Write out John 11:25

_____
_____
_____

### B. What happens at "death"

The human is body, soul and spirit.

- the body is our _____.
- the soul is our _____.
- the spirit is the _____.

What happens to our spirit upon death?

_____

### C. The believer's attitude toward death

According to Philippians 1:21 and 2 Corinthians 5:6-8, how should a believer view death?

_____
_____
_____

### D. The Christian and grief

I Thessalonians 4:13,14

> *"But I do not want you to be ignorant, brethren, concerning those who have fallen asleep, lest you _____."*

What happens to the Christian when he dies?

_____

_____

_____

What attitude should Christians have toward death? Why?

_____

_____

_____

## II. WHAT DOES THE RESSURECTION MEAN TO THE CHRISTIAN

### A. The Resurrection to us is a new birth

What was done for us when Christ was crucified on the Cross?

_____

_____

_____

_____

## B. The resurrection to us is power for each day

According to Ephesians 1:19,20, what message was Paul praying the believers in Ephesus would know?

_____
_____
_____
_____

Write Romans 8:11

_____
_____
_____
_____

## C. The resurrection to us as Christians is a final hope

Why should we not sorrow as those who have no hope?

_____
_____

# IV. THE GENERAL RESURRECTION

What are the two resurrections the Old and New Testament's reference?

_____
_____

Write Romans 9:22

_____
_____
_____

According to 1 Corinthians 15:40-44, what are the changes that will happen in our bodies upon resurrection?

_____
_____
_____
_____

Because of Christ's resurrection from the dead, what "resurrections" are available to us believers? Name and briefly explain each one in your own words.

_____
_____
_____
_____

What is the difference between the body of a believer and the body of a non-believer? *(Romans 9:22 and 1 Cor 15:40-44)*

_____
_____
_____
_____

# Session 2-1
# The Heart of a Man
## God and Man

# The Heart of a Man
Session 1: God and Man

### Answer the following 3 questions:

What are you living for?

_____
_____
_____

What are you prepared to die for?

_____
_____
_____

Have you got what it takes to join God's elite group?

_____
_____
_____

According to the lesson, are men or women more likely to attempt suicide?

_____

According to Proverbs 29:18, why do men seek to end their lives at such high rates?

_____
_____

## Lesson 2-1
### The Heart of a Man 1 - God and Man

What is the essential need of any human being?

_____

What common factors/feelings can draw a person to fulfill an urge to escape through suicide?

_____
_____
_____

One of the telling, very unfortunate traits of the last 2 generations, or fifty years has been the _____ and the rise of _____.

## A compass

How does a child's father act as a compass for their life?

_____
_____
_____
_____
_____
_____

At what ages does a boy need to be affirmed as a young man?

_____

What did the Bible mean when it said we were made in God's image?

_____

_____

_____

There is a _____ heart and there is a _____ heart.

Write the following scriptures

*(Genesis 2:5-7)*

_____

_____

_____

_____

_____

**How does a father shape their child's view of God?**

_____

_____

_____

How does the picture of God's character painted by the scriptures compare to the image that is portrayed in the church today?

_____

_____

_____

_____

_____

_____

# Lesson 2-1
## The Heart of a Man 1 - God and Man

Why do men long for greatness?

_____
_____

What were the differences between the spirit of a man and a woman meant to bring?

_____
_____
_____

# Session 2-2
# Heart of a Man
## Heroes

# Heart of a Man
## Session : Heroes

- Every man wants to be a _____.
- Every child dreams of men as _____.
- Every woman needs her man to be a _____.

What are some of the daily things you can use to redifine "significance?"

_____
_____
_____
_____
_____
_____

Write the definition of the word "hero" as it is stated in the lesson.

_____
_____
_____

Based on the lesson, describe the word "adventure."

_____
_____
_____

What is the bane of Manhood?

_____

# Lesson 2-2
## Heart of a Man 2 - Heroes

What does it mean to be a great lover?

_____
_____
_____


What else do men need besides a battle to fight?

_____
_____


Man is described as the Glory of God. What are women described as in context with creation?

_____

Who holds the answer to helping men reclaim their manhood?

_____

Why do most men usually not attend church?

_____
_____
_____

According to the lesson, what people in American society are the most unchurched?

_____

# Session 3-1
# Your Word is Your Bond
## Your Word

# Your Word is Your Bond
## Session 1: Your Word

What is the difference between a preference and a conviction?

_____
_____
_____

What is the siginificance of benchmarks in a man's life?

_____
_____
_____

Consistency is the testimony of a man's _____.

What are convictions based upon?

_____
_____

What are preferences based upon?

_____
_____

All truth starts as _____, but to become a part of you it must become personal _____. However, only through _____ does truth bring _____. And it is in the transformation of a man that he starts to walk in freedom.

# Lesson 3-1
## Your Word is Your Bond 1 - Your Word

Write John 14:21

_____
_____

No lie can serve the purpose of God, be it internal or verbal. Why is that?

_____
_____
_____

Why is a man's name only as good as his word?

_____
_____
_____

What potential is created in others when we give our word?

_____
_____
_____

What type of man is Psalms 15:4 referring to?

_____
_____
_____

Why is keeping your word a challenge for men today?

_____
_____

Write out Matthew 12:36.

_____
_____
_____

What are idle words?

_____
_____

What is one of the reasons Christians today do not live fulfilled lives?

_____
_____
_____

What does it mean to "trample the truth?"

_____
_____
_____

What is the best thing to do when you have spoken a word in haste or error?

_____
_____
_____

# Session 3-2
# Your Word is Your Bond
## Your Word and Your Family

# Your Word is Your Bond
## Session 2: Your Word and Your Family

How can you teach your children to be flexible while keeping your word?

_____
_____
_____

What is a man giving his word to do when he gives his wedding vows?

_____
_____
_____

Where is a woman's security found?

_____
_____

What is the significance of a woman changing her name in marriage?

_____
_____

What effect can a man's broken word have on a family?

_____
_____
_____

## Lesson 3-2
## Your Word is Your Bond 2 - Your Word and Your Family

How are words the most visible evidence of what is in a man's heart?

_____
_____

What are the three ways we communicate with those around us?

_____

For communication to take place there must be both a _____ and a _____.

What is distortion and what usually causes it?

_____
_____
_____

What happens when communication ceases?

_____
_____

What is the end result of abnormality?

_____

How can abnormailities contaminate a marriage?

_____
_____

How can a man ensure good family relationship in his home?

_____
_____


_____ **give meaning to our words.** What a woman needs from her husband is not just sweet talk, but _____ of love that are accompanied by a sweet willing spirit.

What does communication involve from a husband?

_____
_____
_____


_____ is one of the greatest gifts a man can regularly give his family.


## Spirit to Spirit

What is the most intimate way a man can communicate with his family?

_____

How can praying bring your family closer together?

_____
_____

# Session 4-1
# A Place to Belong
## A Fresh Definition of Church Part 1

# A Place to Belong
## Session 1: A Fresh Definition of Church

Why do most men not value church?

_____
_____
_____

How do men build relationships?

_____
_____
_____

How long does it normally take before a man will call his church "home?"

_____

According to Maslow's Hierarchy, what is the most basic level of need in an individual?

_____

What are the three things that churches need to provide to newcomers to truly give them a desire to serve in the local church?

_____
_____
_____

**LESSON 4-1**
**A PLACE TO BELONG 1 - A FRESH DEFINITION OF CHURCH**

List and define the three things that everyone has to give:

1. _____

   _____

   _____

2. _____

   _____

   _____

3. _____

   _____

   _____

Take some time to answer the following questions.

1. Where do you belong?

   _____

   _____

   _____

2. Have you been neglecting fellowship?

   _____

   _____

   _____

3. Have you seen it as an add-on to your life and not a radical part of it?

   _____

   _____

   _____

4. Do you fellowship with Christ?

5. Do you belong to this house or attend its services?

6. Are you a covenant member or a consuming attendee?

# Session 4-2
# A Place to Belong
A Fresh Definition of Church Part 2

# A Place to Belong
## Session 2: A Fresh Definition of Church Part 2

Define the following terms:

**Committed:** _____
_____

**Consecrated:** _____
_____

**Covenant:** _____
_____

How is the church a collective expression of the inner lives of the saints?
_____
_____
_____

What is a church?
_____
_____
_____

Why did Paul urge every believer not to forsake the gathering together?
_____
_____
_____

# Lesson 4-2
## A Place to Belong 2 - A Fresh Definition of Church Part 2

Write out Genesis 2:18

_____
_____
_____

What is essentially being communicated when someone says they have no need of fellowship?

_____
_____
_____

Why do many Christians not see church and fellowship as essential?

_____
_____

According to the word, what did the early Christians who understood the nature of their call do in their lives as proof of that conviction?

_____
_____
_____

# Session 4-3
# A Place to Belong
## Why Should We Fellowship?

# A Place to Belong
## Session 3: Why Should We Fellowship?

Write Ecclesiasties 4:9-12.

_____
_____
_____

What is the first concept we can grasp from Ecclesiastes 4?

_____
_____
_____

What is the second concept we can grasp from Ecclesiastes 4?

_____
_____
_____

What is the third concept that Ecclesiastes 4 gives us?

_____
_____
_____

# Lesson 4-3
## A Place to Belong 3 - Why Should We Fellowship?

How is the story in Mark 2 a picture of the Body of Christ in perfect harmony?

_____
_____
_____

When does a brother in the faith need you the most?

_____
_____
_____

What is the fourth concept we can find in Ecclesiastes 4?

_____
_____
_____

What is the fifth concept that Ecclesiastes 4 teaches us?

_____
_____
_____

Write Deuteronomy 32:30

_____
_____
_____

What is the sixth concept found in Ecclesiastes 4?

_____
_____
_____


Why do people avoid church and fellowship?

_____
_____
_____

# Session 5-1
# The Imitation of Christ
## Humility Part 1

# The Imitation of Christ
## Session 1: Humility Part 1

*Matt 23: 11-12*

*"But he who is greatest among you shall be your servant. And whoever exalts himself will be humbled, and he who humbles himself will be exalted."*

*Philippians 2:3-6*

*Let nothing be done through selfish ambition or conceit, but in lowliness of mind let each esteem others better than himself. Let each of you look out not only for his own interests, but also for the interests of others. Let this mind be in you which was also in Christ Jesus, who, being in the form of God, did not consider it robbery to be equal with God, but made Himself of no reputation, taking the form of a bondservant, and coming in the likeness of men. And being found in appearance as a man, He humbled Himself and became obedient to the point of death, even the death of the cross. Therefore God also has highly exalted Him and given Him the name, which is above every name.*

What aspect of Christianity is not an aspiration in other beliefs or religions?

_____

What did the Greek philosophy promote?

_____
_____

Define the term Humility.

_____
_____
_____

## Lesson 5-1
### The Imitation of Christ Part 1 - Humility Part 1

What is the definition of pride?

_____
_____
_____


Where does Humility begin?

_____


Write Phillipians 2:3:

_____
_____
_____


What is the focus of this verse?

_____
_____
_____


Write Phillipians 2:5-7

_____
_____
_____

What does it mean to count or esteem others better than yourself?

_____
_____
_____

What should humility be a synonym for?

_____

What does the word "better" mean in the Greek translation?

_____
_____
_____

# Session 5-2
# The Imitation of Christ
## Humility Part 2

# The Imitation of Christ
## Session 2: Humility Part 2

Humility starts in the _____ and continues in _____.

What was the focus of Christ's humility?

_____
_____
_____

What are the five deliberate steps in Christ's actions and patterns of humility that we must be aware of?

1. _____
_____
_____

2. _____
_____

3. _____
_____

4. _____
_____

5. _____

## Lesson 5-2
## The Imitation of Christ Part 2 - Humility Part 2

Humility begins in the _____, continues in _____ and ends in _____.

How did God reward the practice of humility in regards to Jesus?

_____
_____
_____

How is humility indispensable to salvation?

_____
_____
_____

How do we grow in holiness and in Christ-likeness of character and conduct?

_____
_____
_____

List the three benefits that humility brings to our life.

1. _____

2. _____

3. _____

What are six ways you can grow in humility?

1. _____
2. _____
3. _____
4. _____
5. _____
6. _____

# Session 5-3
# The Imitation of Christ
## Generosity

# The Imitation of Christ
## Session 3: Generosity

Write 2 Corinthians 8:8-10.

_____
_____
_____
_____
_____
_____

What does the word "grace" mean?

_____
_____
_____

What four stages did Paul cover when he was writing about grace?

1. _____
2. _____
3. _____
4. _____

What is really meant when the scriptures say that Christ became poor?

_____
_____
_____

# Lesson 5-3
## The Imitation of Christ Part 3 - Generosity

Describe the poverty of man as it is explained in the lesson.

_____
_____
_____

*Eph 3:8*

*To me, who am less than the least of all the saints, this grace was given, that I should* _____
_____,

What are the unspeakable riches that Christ has given to us?

_____
_____

What point did Paul make to the Greek church in 2 Corinthians to persuade them to help the Jewish church?

_____
_____

What are the qualities of authentic Christian giving?

1. _____
2. _____
3. _____
4. _____
5. _____
6. _____
7. _____

# Session 6-1
# Creating a Better Life
## Key #1

# Creating a Better Life
## Session 1: Key #1

What two things must you know in a walk to a better life?

_____
_____
_____

What is the difference between a law and a promise?

_____
_____
_____

What unlocks the promises God has made concerning your life?

_____
_____

Why is it crucial to get your foundations right?

_____
_____
_____

Write Joshua 1:8

_____
_____
_____

# Lesson 6-1
## Creating a Better Life Part 1 - Key #1

What is Key #1 of creating a better life?

_____
_____

Why is this key so important?

_____
_____
_____

Why could God not walk with the children of Israel?

_____
_____
_____

What do words embody?

_____
_____

Why should we practice speaking God's promises into our lives?

_____
_____
_____

# Session 6-2
# Creating a Better Life
## Key #2

# Creating a Better Life
Session 2: Key #2

What is Key #2 in creating a better life?
_____
_____
_____

Write Isaiah 55: 8,9.
_____
_____
_____
_____
_____
_____

Write Romans 12:2
_____
_____
_____

Why was God angry with the Israelites when they did not possess the Promised Land?
_____
_____

# Lesson 6-2
## Creating a Better Life Part 2 - Key #2

What will create new imagery in our mind?

_____
_____
_____


What are the two most powerful things you can do in this life?

_____
_____
_____


How did the image the two spies had differ from that of the remaining ten? What effects did this have?

_____
_____
_____
_____
_____
_____


What is usually absent when wrong thinking is present?

_____


What is required to train oneself to think and speak like God?

_____
_____
_____

# Session 6-3
# Creating a Better Life
## Key #3

# Creating a Better Life
## Session 3: Key #3

What is key #3 to creating a better life?

_____
_____

What is the difference between "wanting" and "cooperating?"

_____
_____
_____

What is a victim mentality?

_____
_____
_____

How can this mentality hinder you in achieving a better life?

_____
_____
_____

# Lesson 6-3
## Creating a Better Life Part 3 - Key #3

In the story of the crippled man by the pool, what was Christ more interested in than his current situation?

_____

_____


When we live our lives according to Joshua 1:8, who will make our lives prosperous?

_____


How does this contrast with the message you have heard regarding a prosperous life?

_____

_____

_____


What three things must we leave behind to achieve our better life?

_____

_____

_____

# Session 7-1
# Character is King
## God Created You for Excellence

# Character is King
Session 1: God Created You for Excellence

Define the term "Workmanship."
_____
_____
_____

What does "Good Works" mean?
_____

What does God reserve for those who reverence Him?
_____
_____
_____

Write Romans 12:6.
_____
_____

## Lesson 7-1
### Character is King Part 1 - God Created You for Excellence

Why is it a myth to believe that we will be ok if we focus on improving our weaknesses?

_____
_____
_____


What must we do to accomplish what God has created us to do?

_____
_____


What is the result of focusing on our weaknesses?

_____
_____


Answer the following four questions to determine your strengths.

1. What am I good at?

   _____
   _____
   _____


2. What do I enjoy doing?

   _____
   _____
   _____

3. What have others said I do well?

___

4. Where have I seen rapid learning or glimpses of excellence?

___

# Session 7-2
# Character is King
Faithfulness - The Very Character of God

# Character is King
## Session 2: Faithfulness - The Very Character of God

Write Psalm 89:8.

_____
_____
_____

What does God prize above every other character attribute?

_____

What is the difference between reputation and character?

_____
_____
_____

What mistake do men make when they are making a decision regarding a person?

_____
_____
_____

# Lesson 7-2
## Character is King Part 2 - Faithfulness - The Very Character of God

Write Luke 16: 10-12.

What things must we do before we will be entrusted with more?

Write the following scriptures.

Zechariah 4:10

Job 8:7

Luke 16:11-12

___
___
___

# Session 7-3
# Character is King
## God Has Anointed You for Business

# Character is King
## Session 3: God Has Anointed You for Business

In what ways are the Kingdom of God run like a business?

_____
_____
_____

How much of Jesus' teaching was focused on money and finances?

_____

What type of people did Jesus choose as his disciples?

_____
_____
_____

What is the central issue that all Christians should focus on?

_____
_____

# Lesson 7-2
## Character is King Part 3 - God Has Anointed You for Business

# Write the following scriptures.

1 John 2:20
_____
_____


1 John 2:27
_____
_____
_____


What was the purpose and anointing of the following offices in the Old Testament?

Prophet
_____
_____


Priest
_____
_____
_____


King
_____
_____
_____

What is the purpose of anointing in our lives?

_____
_____
_____


What does the anointing of God represent?

_____
_____
_____

# Session 8-1
# Marriage and Family
## Different from the Start

# Marriage and Family
## Session 1: Different From the Start

What was the purpose of the differences between men and women?

_____
_____
_____

According to the lesson, where was Adam created and how does it reflect upon his character as a man?

_____
_____
_____
_____

Where was Eve created and how does it reflect the character that God gave to her?

_____
_____
_____
_____
_____

# Lesson 8-1
## Marriage and Family Part 1 - Different From the Start

Why did God create Eve from Adam instead of making a brand new creation altogether?

_____
_____
_____

How does a man allow his wife to be his glory?

_____

How do many men make mistakes when dealing with women?

_____
_____
_____

Where is a man's inner desire to take dominion satisfied?

_____
_____

Why can most men be satisifed with just having a job and a good sexual relationship at home?

_____
_____
_____

Why is procreation never evidence of maturity?
_____
_____

In view of God's creation process, how are women supposed to be viewed and treated?
_____
_____

How has that image been corrupted in today's culture?
_____
_____

# Session 8-2
# Marriage and Family
## The Sacredness of Sex

# Marriage and Family
## Session 2: The Sacredness of Sex

What must we first understand before we can understand the importance of sex?

_____
_____
_____

What is a covenant?

_____
_____

What were the purposes of covenants between families?

_____
_____

What did it mean to enter into a blood covenant in Abram's time?

_____
_____
_____

# Lesson 8-2
## Marriage and Family Part 2 - The Sacredness of Sex

How were the animals in a covenant ceremony prepared?

_____
_____
_____

What was the first thing the parties involved in covenant did, and what did it represent?

_____
_____
_____
_____

What was the second thing that parties involved in covenant did?  Explain its significance.

_____
_____
_____
_____
_____

What was the third step of covenant and what did it symbolize?

_____
_____
_____
_____
_____
_____

What was the fourth custom of covenant and what did it represent?

_____
_____
_____
_____
_____
_____

What was the final step involved with making covenants?

_____
_____
_____

What had to take place for a covenant to be seen as ratified and immortalized?

_____

## Lesson 8-2
## Marriage and Family Part 2 - The Sacredness of Sex

What was the sign of the covenant between man and God in the Old Testament?

_____

What was the sign of the covenant between man and God in the New Testament?

_____

What are circumcision and communion symbolic of?

_____

What part does sex play in the covenant process of marriage?

_____
_____

What is the significance of our virginity?

_____
_____

In the marriage relationship, who holds the power of sex?

_____


Why did God make sex good?

_____

_____

# Session 8-3
# Marriage and Family
## What's the Big Deal With Pornography

# Marriage and Family
Session 3: What's the Big Deal With Pornography

What is the difference between lust and love?

_____
_____
_____

What is pornography created to do?

_____
_____
_____

What does the word "pornography" mean?

_____
_____
_____

What must a judge determine before something can be labeled as "obscene" and unprotected by the First Amendment?

_____
_____
_____

## Lesson 8-2
## Marriage and Family Part 3 - What's the Big Deal With Pornography

What is the lie that pornography portrays?

_____
_____

How is pornography a counterfeit for prayer?

_____
_____
_____

Write Proverbs 7:24-27

_____
_____
_____
_____
_____
_____

What could be the "harlot of King Solomon's time" in today's society?

_____
_____
_____

# Session 8-4
# Marriage and Family
## The Process of Pornography

# Marriage and Family
Session 4: The Process of Pornography

What is phase one of pornography?
_____

What effects do epinephrine have on a man?
_____
_____
_____

How can we "trash" the images that come at us?
_____
_____
_____

What is phase two of pornography?
_____

# Lesson 8-4
## Marriage and Family Part 4 - The Process of Pornography

What is involved in this phase?

_____
_____
_____

What signs can tell you when pornography has become an idol to a man?

_____
_____
_____
_____
_____
_____

What is phase three of pornography?

_____
_____

What is a man's mind supposed to be?

_____
_____

What can pornography do to a man's life in this phase?

_____
_____


What is phase four of pornography?

_____


What does this phase look like?

_____
_____
_____


Where does pornography ultimately lead to?

_____


What do you do if you are caught in the cycle of pornography?

_____
_____
_____

# Session 8-5
# Marriage and Family
Freedom From the Effects of Pornography

# Marriage and Family
Session 5: Freedom From the Effects of Pornography

What are the 12 areas of personal responsibility when dealing with pornography?

1. _____
2. _____
3. _____
4. _____
5. _____
6. _____
7. _____
8. _____
9. _____
10. _____
11. _____
12. _____

What is the greatest thing you will have to do to overcome the sin of pornography?
_____

# Lesson 8-5
## Marriage and Family Part 5 - Freedom From the Effects of Pornography

List the 10 things you should incorporate into your life when dealing with pornography.

1. _____
2. _____
3. _____
4. _____
5. _____
6. _____
7. _____
8. _____
9. _____
10. _____

# Session 8-6
# Marriage and Family
## Fatherhood

# Marriage and Family
## Session 6: Fatherhood

What does a mother provide to a child?

_____

What does a father provide to a child?

_____

What effect does it have on a child when the father is taken out of his/her life?

_____
_____

Based on the statistics in the teaching, how would you say a child is impacted by the absense of a father?

_____
_____
_____

## Lesson 8-6
## Marriage and Family Part 6 - Fatherhood

What does it really mean to be a father?

_____
_____
_____

What effect has been produced by the lack of appropriate male models today?

_____
_____
_____

If you have not been an appropriate model of a father to your children, what are some steps you can take to begin dealing with the situation?

_____
_____
_____

# Session 8-7
# Marriage and Family
## 6 Keys to Raising Children

# Marriage and Family
Session 7: 6 Keys to Raising Children

What is the first key to raising children?
_____

What is involved in this key?
_____
_____
_____
_____
_____
_____

What is the second key to raising children?
_____

What is involved in this key?
_____
_____
_____

# Lesson 8-7
## Marriage and Family Part 7 - 6 Keys to Raising Children

What is key number three in raising children?

_____

What is lasciviousness, and how does it affect the world?

_____
_____
_____

What form of actions would be considered lascivious?

_____
_____
_____

What is key number four to raising children?

_____

Why do you have to be a role model to your child?

_____
_____
_____

What is key number five to raising children?
_____

What does this entail?
_____
_____
_____

What could be labeled as a "home invader" and why?
_____
_____
_____

What is the sixth key to raising children?
_____

What is involved in this step?
_____
_____
_____

# Session 8-8
# Marriage and Family
## 7 Keys to Family Discipline

# Marriage and Family
Session 8: 7 Keys to Family Discipline

What does the equation A+B+C=D stand for?
_____
_____
_____

Why is consistency important when raising children?
_____
_____
_____

What is the first key to family discipline?
_____
_____

How is this the origin of so many discipline problems today?
_____
_____
_____

# Lesson 8-8
## Marriage and Family Part 8 - 7 Keys to Family Discipline

What is the second key to family discipline?
_____
_____

What questions should you ask yourself before you discipline your children?
_____
_____
_____

What is the third key to raising children?
_____
_____

What should your corrections cause your children to do?
_____
_____

What is the fourth key to family discipline?
_____
_____

What is key number five in family discipline?

_____
_____

What is key number six in family discipline?

_____
_____

What is key number seven in family discipline?

_____
_____

Why should you not discipline your children out of anger?

_____
_____
_____

# Session 8-9
# Marriage and Family
Creating Your Child's Character

# Marriage and Family
Session 9: Creating Your Child's Character

What are some of the differences between a coach and a father?

_____
_____
_____
_____
_____
_____

What is a father?

_____
_____
_____

How can the environment your child is raised in affect their ability to face the world?

_____
_____
_____

# Lesson 8-9
## Marriage and Family Part 9 - Creating Your Childs Character

What is meant when the phrase "monkey see, monkey do" is used to describe the example you give your kids?

_____
_____
_____

Why is it important that you allow your children to see you do things like apologize, ask forgiveness, and deal with life's everyday situations?

_____
_____
_____

How can modeling reconciliation to your children help them in the future?

_____
_____
_____

# Session 9-1
# Achieving Authentic Wealth
## Preparing For Wealth

# Achieving Authentic Wealth
Session 1: Preparing For Wealth

What causes men to use the money they have on self-consumption?
_____

What happens when someone doesn't have a dream or a revelation for their life?
_____
_____
_____

What sort of vision does the church today need?
_____
_____
_____

According to Ecclesiastes 5:10-11, what does the future look like for those who are on a path of "self-consumption?"
_____
_____
_____

# Lesson 9-1
## Achieving Authentic Wealth Part 1 - Preparing For Wealth

What does the phrase "wealth hoarded" mean?

_____
_____
_____

What does it really mean to "take over" our land of promise, and how has it been misrepresented in today's culture?

_____
_____
_____

What is ignorance?

_____
_____
_____

What picture does the "vegetable garden" show us in regards to mentality?

_____
_____
_____

What does the word "need" mean in Phillipians 4:19?

_____
_____
_____

How does God provide for these needs?

_____
_____
_____

# Session 9-2
# Achieving Authentic Wealth
## Multiplying Money Into Wealth

# Achieving Authentic Wealth
## Session 2: Multiplying Money Into Wealth

What is wealth?

_____
_____
_____

According to Jesus, what is the most important duty of a man in his life?

_____
_____

What separates supernatural success from prosperity?

_____
_____

What are God's new requirements for us?

_____
_____

## Lesson 9-2
### Achieving Authentic Wealth Part 2 - Multiplying Money Into Wealth

What should you use to measure yourself?

_____

What happens when we love, serve, and obey God?

_____

What is the difference between a Godly prosperity message and man's prosperity message?

_____

What is the foremost passion of God?

_____

What does it mean to understand the heartbeat of God?

_____

# Session 9-3
# Achieving Authentic Wealth
## How To Lose Your Wealth

# Achieving Authentic Wealth
## Session 3: How To Lose Your Wealth

How do we restrict God's very best toward us?

_____
_____
_____

What is God's response when we focus on things that keep us from His best?

_____
_____
_____

What does God desire the foundation of our life to be and why?

_____
_____
_____

What is more important than outward prosperity?

_____

# Lesson 9-3
## Achieving Authentic Wealth Part 3 - How To Lose Your Wealth

What is the greatest threat to our God-given wealth and prosperity?
_____
_____

What controls our life and how does it rob us?
_____

What does unsanctified money, success, and power do in our life?
_____
_____
_____

How does debt steal control of our lives?
_____
_____
_____

How has society's culture crept into our theology?
_____
_____
_____

How has compromise set into the church, and what effect has it had?

_____
_____
_____

# Session 9-4
# Achieving Authentic Wealth
## The Real Purpose of Wealth

# Achieving Authentic Wealth
## Session 4: The Real Purpose of Wealth

How is love expressed toward God?

_____
_____
_____

What is God's ultimate purpose and plan in the earth?

_____
_____
_____

Why is financial wealth given to us?

_____
_____
_____

What does it mean to dispossess the nations?

_____
_____

# Lesson 9-4
## Achieving Authentic Wealth Part 4 - The Real Purpose of Wealth

Why do we need a vision greater than anything we can possibly execute on our own?

_____
_____
_____


What stops so many Christians, particularly in the western world, from beginning to do the work that God has given them to do?

_____
_____
_____


What must we do in order to "dispossess the nations?"

_____
_____
_____


Why is the fight to spread the gospel not for the religious, good person, or the novice Christian?

_____
_____
_____

When does the enemy aggressively attack and sometimes defeat us?

_____
_____


What happens when people keep feeding their appetites?

_____
_____
_____

# Session 9-5
# Achieving Authentic Wealth
## Consider Abraham Part 1

# Achieving Authentic Wealth
Session 5: Consider Abraham Part 1

In looking at your life, how can you see the same process unfolding as it did in Abraham's life?

_____
_____
_____

What happened when Abraham passed by landmarkers?

_____
_____
_____

What are the lessons you can gather from the story of Abraham's wandering?

_____
_____
_____
_____
_____
_____

# Lesson 9-5
## Achieving Authentic Wealth Part 5 - Consider Abraham Part 1

Write Romans 8:29

_____
_____
_____

What does the term "predestine" mean?

_____
_____

Why can you not stay attached to the world, its systems, and its culture?

_____
_____

What can we learn from Haran?

_____
_____
_____

What must die in our lives as we journey toward being a blessing?

_____

How can we take responsibility for our maturity?

According to Abraham's example, what should we do when we go through a place of destruction or devastation in our lives?

What was the purpose of Abraham going through the Negev?

What do people usually do when they come to their "Negev?"

What will your experience in the Negev do for you?

# Session 9-6
# Achieving Authentic Wealth
## Consider Abraham Part 2

# Achieving Authentic Wealth
## Session 6: Consider Abraham Part 2

How is Egypt a type of "the world" in the Bible?

_____
_____
_____


Why did God send Abraham to Egypt? What was He trying to teach him?

_____
_____
_____


What three things did Abraham acquire while in Egypt?

_____
_____
_____


Once you are in your established career path, how will you learn what you need to know?

_____
_____

# Lesson 9-6
## Achieving Authentic Wealth Part 6 - Consider Abraham Part 2

How did Abraham acquire his assets?

What is the biblical formula for financial success?

Why is it important for you to maintain a personal relationship with God in a worldly market?

Why do we not need to "make camp" and wait for God in a location?

What is the purpose of the church?

How can a church have no financial problems?

_____
_____


How did Abraham prove that ministry people and business people can work together to accomplish one goal?

_____
_____
_____


What is our purpose as the church of Christ?

_____
_____
_____

# Session 9-7
# Achieving Authentic Wealth
## Consider Abraham Part 3

# Achieving Authentic Wealth
Session 7: Consider Abraham Part 3

What observations can be made regarding Abrahams confrontation with Lot?

_____
_____
_____
_____
_____
_____

What factors made Lot choose the easy way?

_____
_____
_____

What were the consequences of that choice?

_____
_____
_____
_____
_____
_____

## Lesson 9-7
## Achieving Authentic Wealth Part 7 - Consider Abraham Part 3

What are the vital things we choose daily that determine our commitment and blessings?

_____
_____
_____

What does prosperity really entail?

_____
_____
_____

What traits qualified Abraham to be the steward and distributor of God's blessing?

_____
_____

What two things did Abraham possess that he was blessed with to redistribute to the world outside of who he was, his knowledge, wisdom, and character?

_____
_____
_____

# Resources of Interest

**Character is King**
*Dr. John Binkley*

It's a Guy Thing: Character is King takes you on your dream journey. There is a place called destiny that we all journey to. We all have ideas, dreams and vision for what life should be. This book lays out a plan for that journey to realizing your dreams, to your destiny.

**Let's Talk About Sex**
*Dr. John A. King*

Let's face it. Sexuality is all around us. It's even on billboards, and television commercials. Sadly, It's a topic many men have to discover on their own because too many churches or pastors won't touch it. *Let's Talk About Sex* was written so men no longer have to discover the answers to the tough questions about sex on their own.

**Now to Next**
*Dr. John A. King*

What does the next generation church look like? Who are the people that will be involved in the next generation church? How will it come about?

Those are some of the questions answered in Dr. King's newest release, *Now to Next: Blueprint for a Christian Revolution*.

**Helping Guys Become Men, Husbands, and Fathers**
*Dr. John A. King*

It's a Guy Thing takes you on the journey of fatherhood. Dr. King shows you, in this book, the skills necessary to become a good father. He shows you what can happen when a father is absent or simply not active in a child's life. Being a male is a matter of birth. Being a man is a matter of choice. This book will help you make that choice.

To see all the titles available through Guy Thing Press, visit us online at www.guythingpress.com

# Resources of Interest

**Business By The Book**
*Dr. John A. King*

The world's greatest handbook on leadership, economic and social excellence is not found in schoolbooks, but is Scripture. The principles in this book are tried, proven and resilient over centuries. Christ bet His life on it, and so can you.

**Show Me the Money**
*Dr. John A. King*

Time Magazine asked, "Does God want you to be rich?" The answer to that question is simply "No, God wants you to be *wealthy*." In *Show Me the Money*, you will learn the fundamentals of creating and using wealth in God's kingdom.

**Achieving Authentic Wealth**
*Jeff McLoud*

We need a vision that goes beyond our ability to be consumers only. A vision so big, so powerful, that we cannot even accomplish it in our own lifetime - a vision founded from the very heartbeat of God. We could see the vision fulfilled if we ask ourselves a simple question: "How can we achieve twice as much with half the money?"

**Creating a Better Life**
*Erik A. Kudlis*

In this easy to read manual, educator and administrator turned national and international businessman, Erik Kudlis, identifies three vital keys you must know and use, given by God Himself, that unlock the doors to the life God always wanted you to have.

To see all the titles available through Guy Thing Press, visit us online at www.guythingpress.com

# Further Resources

### The Godly Man Curriculum

The Godly Man Curriculum is the latest development of the International Men's Network. This training curriculum is designed to train men from all walks of life and give them a firm foundation of doctrine and Godly knowledge. This curriculum is available both over the internet for individual study or by DVD for seminars, Sunday schools, and men's meetings. With up to 7 hours of video teaching divided over numerous topics, the Godly Man Curriculum is an excellent tool that you can build your classes upon and grow yourself and your people.

### Building Iron Men & Life As Leaders Networks

The Building Iron Men and Life as Leaders networks are two of IMN's finest resources. Each network provides you with a new teaching every month that will challenge and encourage you to grow. The Building Iron Men network features three teachings in both CD and DVD format that focus on your men, while the Life as Leaders network provides you with three CDs that teach you leadership principles you can use in every area of your life.

Both networks are phenomenal tools that are vital assets to any church and discipleship program.

For more information about these and other resources, visit us online at www.imnonline.org

## Also check out these websites for great resources and training materials.

International Men's Network
www.imnonline.org

Guy Thing Press
www.guythingpress.com

The International Men's Network was founded by Dr. John A. King. Our purpose as an organization is to help men not only grow to become the leaders their families and churches need, but also become men of God that make a lasting impact on those around them.

IMN is a missionary organization to the men of the world. We are committed to:

- Inspire all men to rise to a high standard of biblical manhood.
- Encourage them to excel in their roles as men, leaders, husbands, and fathers.
- Challenge them to be contributors to society and set an example based upon a Biblical value system that will benefit this generation and lay a solid foundation for the next.

As an organization, the International Men's Network is dedicated to providing and hosting the best resources for men, whether it comes from teachings and lessons on CD/DVD format or via a conference that will teach men principles that will help them become more influential and effective in their lives.

For more information about IMN and its mission, visit us online at www.imnonline.org or contact us via phone at 817.993.0047

The Christian Life Center was founded by Dr. John King and his wife, Beccy. With a vision to preach the gospel of Jesus Christ with unashamed passion and uncompromising truth, Christian Life Center aims to raise up the next generation of leaders to move into all the world and proclaim the truth of Christ to the lost and broken.

Located in the Keller, TX area, the Church sits in the prime location to reach the community and the people therein. The Church desires to give back to the community by providing outreaches to better and enrich its inhabitants. From kickboxing classes that are aimed at teaching children and adults self-defense to special service that commemorate and honor our country's war-time heroes, the church strives to bring a living Jesus to a dying world by new and imaginative means that will bless and change lives.

For more information about Christian Life Center and the resources it offers, visit the website at www.clctx.org